CW00326532

THE COUNTRY
PRESERVES COMPANION

THE COUNTRY
PRESERVES COMPANION

JOCASTA INNES
PHOTOGRAPHY BY JAMES MERRELL

MITCHELL BEAZLEY

THE COUNTRY PRESERVES COMPANION
Jocasta Innes

First published in Great Britain 1995
by Mitchell Beazley
an imprint of Reed Consumer Books Limited
Michelin House, 81 Fulham Road, London SW3 6RB
and Auckland, Melbourne, Singapore and Toronto

Photography by *James Merrell*
Illustrations by *Michael Hill*

Art Editor *Trinity Fry*
Editor *Jennifer Jones*
Art Director *Jacqui Small*
Executive Editor *Judith More*
Production *Heather O'Connell*

A CIP record for this book is available from the British Library

ISBN 1 85732 450 1

The publishers have made every effort to ensure that all instructions given in this book are accurate and safe,
but they cannot accept liability for any resulting injury, damage or loss to either person or property,
whether direct or consequential and howsoever arising. The authors and publishers will be grateful
for any information which will assist them in keeping future editions up to date.

Colour reproduction by Rival Colour, UK
Produced by Mandarin Offset. Printed and bound in China

CONTENTS

Introduction   6

THE PRESERVES KITCHEN

Equipment   10

Bottling Techniques   16

How to Prepare Ingredients   18

Jars & Storage   20

Presentation   24

COUNTRY PRESERVES RECIPES

Marmalades, Jams & Jellies   28

Pickles & Chutneys   43

Bottled Fruit & Vegetables   56

Index   64

INTRODUCTION

The art of preserving good fresh food is at least as old as the art of cookery itself – of which, of course, it is a noble branch. Until very recent times a glance into any larder would have told a satisfying tale of thrifty labours – of subtle blends of spice and fruits; of steaming pots, and brimming ladles; of a kitchen garden carefully tended and of pleasant trips into the countryside in spring and autumn, basket in hand, to gather mushrooms and berries – the ranks of bottles and jars twinkling with promise of imminent reward.

In an age when a lot of food can be simply stuffed into a freezer, you might ask whether making preserves is worth the trouble. Food out of the freezer comes out as it went in, and mostly still needs cooking; preserves, on the other hand, may mellow and ripen over the months and emerge ready to eat. What is really preserved, in bottles and jars and stoneware crocks, under airtight lids, is wonderful country cooking, its pleasures heightened by being deferred.

The subtle changes to the raw ingredients used in the recipes in this book cannot be achieved in any other way. You can freeze an orange, certainly, but all you get is a sorry, soggy orange: but in a freshly opened jar of home-made marmalade you have something rich and rare.

THE PRESERVES KITCHEN

EQUIPMENT

Some of the recipes in this book require next to no specialised equipment, and even for the jams a heavy-based saucepan and a wooden spoon may be adequate. But if you are planning to cook in any quantity, you will find it useful to invest in a large preserving pan, with handle and pouring lip, containing anything between 6 and 9 litres (1½ and 2 gallons). This may seem more than you could manage but it is a good idea to keep the pan only half-full, at the most; otherwise boiling sugar can foam and overflow in a moment. Preserving pans are relatively wide and shallow, designed to help evaporation, and shelve gradually outwards towards the lip, like buckets.

The best preserving pans are made of heavy-gauge stainless steel, with a really heavy base to spread the heat; and they are expensive. You can find cheaper versions, down to enamelled iron and non-stick aluminium, but the internal coating must be perfect. Plain aluminium should be avoided; and old copper or brass pans are no good for pickles: the vinegar will leach out the metallic salts and flavour the preserve horribly.

You will need a set of scales, of course, and a battery of wooden spoons, preferably cut on the slant for stirring the bottom of the pan, with long handles to keep your fingers away from boiling sugar as it spits and heaves.

To tell, infallibly, when the jam is set, a jam-making thermometer is very useful; as are a wide-spouted jam funnel and a jug for transferring the scalding produce into the jars without spills or tears. You will need a fine nylon or stainless steel sieve, a stainless steel or enamelled ladle, and a lemon squeezer. Sooner or later you will want muslin for straining jellies and for keeping herbs and spices, pips and peel, separate from the mixture in your pan. The prefabricated jelly bags sold in kitchenware shops do the job without fiddle.

Of course you need a chopping board – and the bigger the better. Boards for carving joints, with a gutter around the edge for catching the juices, are ideal. Plastic or vinyl boards are clean and very light; but you may prefer, as I do, a thick wooden board with some 'feel' to it, and to sweep the fruit off it into a pan held underneath.

Nothing beats the knife you like, as long as it is sharp. Itinerant chefs carry their own around with them, and once you have a knife that suits you, hang on to it. It should preferably be of stainless steel, and the better quality stainless knives will take sharpening with a steel or whetstone so that they cut swiftly and cleanly, without pulling or leaving ragged

edges. Food processors can be used to save time, but be warned: they will not do much for either the texture or appearance of your preserves. Most preserves will keep for months or even years: a few extra minutes at the start using a knife and board is worthwhile.

A paring knife with a swivel head will come in handy when peeling large quantities of apples. An apple coring device saves time, too, although if your apples are very large you should check that it has done the job properly. A paring knife will also zest lemons, but I find my small steel kitchen knife is sharper and more satisfying to use, leaving the pith behind.

How you choose to pot your preserves depends on you: the only criterion is that the seal should be perfect. Old jam jars, new jars with clip down rubber sealing rings, stoneware crocks, all will do; but unless your family is very large, 450 g (1 lb) containers are the most suitable size. You will need wax paper, perhaps a clear preserving film, elastic bands and labels, all of which you can buy in a single packet. Unless you really enjoy cleaning up, a pile of old newspapers, for spreading almost everywhere, is invaluable.

And if all this sounds daunting, remember that our forbears made do with earthen crocks, wooden spoons and an iron pan!

One last thought: never be afraid of making too much. Most of the recipes in this book provide for a decent amount – say six or eight jars; but preserves dealt with glut, and were intended to be made on a grand scale. Provided you have the jars and a big enough pan, making more jam does not mean more complication You aren't preparing an elaborate dinner party, and only you need know if anything goes wrong.

BOTTLING TECHNIQUES

Jars and bottles, and their lids and corks too, should be scrupulously clean: wash them in warm soapy water, rinse, then boil for half an hour and finally dry them off in a preheated oven at 110°C (225°F, gas mark ¼) for a good hour. Muslin should be scalded before use.

Jams and jellies, chutneys and pickles should all be sealed when either hot or cold, but never when tepid. Fill the jars to within 5 mm (¼ in) of the rim. Place a circle of wax paper on the surface of the jam, smoothing out any trapped air bubbles, and seal.

All pickles, fruit sauces, ketchups and bottled fruits must be sterilized in the bottle to prevent fermentation. Fill the bottles to within 2.5 cm (1 in) of the top, and seal lightly with a cork or screw-top cap. The easiest method is to place the loosely sealed jars in a preheated oven at 150°C (300°F, gas mark 2) for 40–60 minutes, depending on the solidity of the contents, and then screw down the lids tightly. A vacuum will form when the mixture cools; but the preserve will not keep as long as by the water-bath method. For this, put a trivet in a big pan or line the base with a folded cloth, stand the bottles in place, and fill the pan with water to reach their necks. Let the water boil vigorously for at least 15 minutes, then carefully remove the bottles and secure the cap or cork tightly.

HOW TO PREPARE INGREDIENTS

The essential ingredients in preserves are sugar and salt, vinegar and oil. You can get special 'preserving sugar' that dissolves quickly, but what you have in the cupboard will do. Use brown sugar where specified as this gives a distinctive and stronger flavour. For chutneys and sauces, you may find it useful to keep at hand a jar of preserved stem ginger, and a packet of crystallized ginger, too. Spice is, of course, the soul of a good chutney, in the right combination, so your rack should include soft spices — cloves, nutmeg, cinnamon and cardamom — for soft fruits and fiery flavours — chillies, peppercorns and mustard seeds — for piquant preserves. It is a myth that preserves can be made with the worst of a crop — in fact, the opposite is generally true. It is the slightly unripe fruit that makes the best jam. Blemishes can introduce unwanted undertones to the flavour, and fruit used for bottling or preserving should be at the peak of condition. Try to avoid squashing your blackberries or dropping your apples: once the skin is broken, unwelcome yeasts will start to form.

The old saw *an hour from the garden to the pot* still holds true, even if an hour is rather going it. In fact, you should aim to give yourself a clear run — a whole afternoon, or evening (many fruits are best picked in early evening), without other distractions.

18

JARS & STORAGE

You can rush out and invest in a raft of glass preserving jars with rubber seals, but the essence of country preserving is an abhorrence of waste. The country cook will save jam jars and useful bottles throughout the year, and the eclectic range of shapes and sizes adds to the Ali Baba delight of a well-stocked larder or cupboard. Vinegar-based preserves like chutneys and pickles begin to dry out as soon as they are opened, so the traditional shape of a chutney jar is tall and thin; jam jars, on the other hand, may be round and fat, perhaps to denote the sugar they contain. Old stoneware and crockery jars are nice in principle but dodgy if the glaze is cracked or crazed. French mustard can be bought in wide-mouthed stoneware jars with a big cork. When empty, remove the old wax in very hot water. Sterilise as usual, fill it with your preserve and heat sterilise if necessary, then hammer the cork in tightly and seal by dipping the head of the jar into hot paraffin wax, to prevent any air reaching the contents.

What is crucial is the quality of the seal: even oil becomes rancid if exposed to air. A perfectly good way to keep a jar of jam or chutney air-tight is to run a spoonful of melted paraffin wax (candle-ends will do) over an initial paper seal. Let the wax solidify, and then repeat the process. If you are re-using old lids, examine the plastic coating on the inside and

you are re-using old lids, examine the plastic coating on the inside and throw away any that are rusted or pitted, for vinegar will eat through bare metal in no time. Lidless jars may be sealed with a proprietary cellophane that shrinks when wetted, and secured with a rubber band: a small circle of cotton placed over the top and tied with ribbon adds a finishing touch. Jams and chutneys make excellent presents.

Up to the moment that you pot your preserves, sun and air are your allies; from then on your paths diverge. They now look to rot what they've ripened, and you must keep your jars and bottles away from them. Most of the following preserves should be kept dry, in the cool, away from direct sunlight – in the old-fashioned country larder, ideally, along with the cheeses, puddings and cold meats that refrigerators invariably spoil. Most of us, however, will have to make do with a cupboard under the stairs, or a lower kitchen cabinet: anywhere that is cool, dry and dark.

Most home-made marmalades, jams, jellies and chutneys will last for at least 6 months, and many will last a year or more. Unfortunately, storage dates on home-made produce cannot be an exact science, so if you want to be absolutely sure, eat within 6 months. Once the jar has been opened, store it in the refrigerator and eat within 2 weeks. Pickles, relishes and bottled fruit and vegetables have a much shorter shelf-life of 6 weeks. Once opened, keep the jars in the refrigerator and consume within 1 week – not usually too difficult!

PRESENTATION

Once the jars or bottles are sealed and wiped clean, it goes without saying that they should be labelled. Labels can be as plain or elaborate as you like, but should always record the date on which the preserve was made, and a full description of the contents.

Sauce bottles tend to have dull plastic screw-top lids, associated with the manufacturer of the original ketchup or sauce, but the bottles can be enlivened if you whittle down a wine cork to fit the hole tightly. Boil the cork, like any other bottle top, for 20 minutes to soften and sterilise it. Once the cork is in place, melt some coloured wax in a pan and dip the bottle top into it for a foolproof seal.

Home-made gifts from the kitchen really are valued as they convey so much more than something you just go out and pay for, and there is no end of fancying up that can go on the outside of the jar. Use scraps of fabric for decorative lid covers, and secure them with coloured ribbons tied into a bow. Or melt down a coloured candle (see above), seal the bottle or jar, and press anything embossed – a coin, a butter mould, a brass button – into the wax as it cools, as a formal seal. Turn your labels into works of art with watercolours or crayons, or try pasting on pressed flowers (of the correct season, of course).

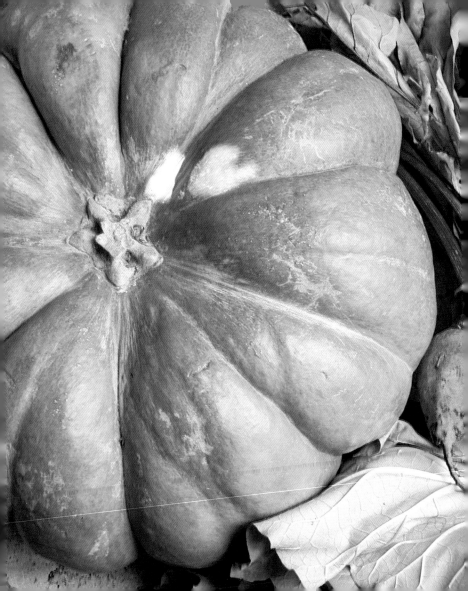

COUNTRY PRESERVES RECIPES

MARMALADES, JAMS & JELLIES

Pectin and sugar are the requisites for a good set. Fruits high in pectin (cooking apples, blackcurrants, plums, gooseberries, red currants and quinces) combine with more sugar to produce more jam; fruits low in pectin (strawberries, late blackberries, cherries and pears) and vegetables use less sugar, and make less jam.

Jellies are clear and translucent; they are best made with tart fruit, such as crab apples and damsons, and may be flavoured with herbs. Simmer the fruit until it is soft, then suspend the pulp in a jelly bag to strain into a clean bowl overnight. Do not squeeze the bag, or the jelly will be cloudy. Measure the juice, add the same quantity of sugar, and boil until set.

It is a good idea to simmer the fruit to a pulp before adding sugar, but once the sugar is in, a vigorous boil tends to keep the colour bright and prevents darkening. Once on the boil, jams will set between 10 and 15 minutes. To test for set, use a jam thermometer, which comes ready graded, with the setting temperatures of jam marked off. As an alternative, place a drop of the boiling jam onto a clean saucer, blow to cool, and push it with your fingertip. If it smears easily across the plate, the jam is still too runny. Boil for a few moments, and repeat the test. As soon as the drop of jam crinkles under your finger, it is ready.

Seville marmalade

Seville Marmalade

*Glut is here the mother of invention; and
Mrs Keiller, whose husband had rashly
bought up a shipload of these bitter oranges
in Dundee, hit upon this method of using
them up: an enduring marriage of Spanish
prodigality and Scottish thrift.*

2 lb (900 g) Seville oranges
4 pints (2.25 litres) water
juice of 1 large lemon
4 lb (1.75 kg) sugar

Wash the oranges and put them in a
large saucepan with the water. Cook
over a low heat for about 2 hours,
until the peel can easily be pierced
with a fork. Take the oranges out of
the pan and when cool enough to
handle, cut them up, in thick or fine
shreds, saving all the pips. Put the fruit
into a preserving pan. Tie the pips in
a muslin bag, and add this to the
cooking liquid in the saucepan, with
the lemon juice. Boil for 5 minutes.
Strain the liquid, add it to the shred-
ded fruit and boil until the mixture is
reduced by one third. Add the sugar,
stir to dissolve, then bring to the boil
and boil fast until setting point is
reached. Cool briefly, stir, and pot.

Grapefruit Marmalade

*Marmalades and marmalets were made of
citrus fruits long before Mrs Keiller; this is
one made since her death, with the waspish
zing of grapefruit.*

3 grapefruit
4 lemons
4 pints (2.25 litres) water
3 lb (1.5 kg) sugar

Peel the fruit quite finely so that as
much pith as possible is left, then
remove the pith. Set aside the peel and
pith. Cut the fruit in half and remove
the seeds. Put these with the thick pith
from the grapefruit into a muslin bag.
Chop the fruit roughly on a plate to
save the juice. Shred all the peel finely. Put everything into a preserving
pan with the water and simmer until
soft – about 1½ hours. Remove the
muslin bag, squeezing out any liquid.
Stir in the sugar, bring to the boil and
proceed as for Seville Marmalade.

COUNTRY PRESERVES RECIPES

Gooseberry Jam

*One of the easiest jams to make, as goose-
berries have a high pectin content and set
readily. If you like a slightly tart jam, then
it is also one of the nicest. Unripe gooseberries are best for jam as their skins are less
tough. If you can, cook the berries in a copper preserving pan so that they keep their
green colour – otherwise they will turn a
pinkish-amber shade. The marriage of
gooseberries and elderflowers is an old one:
a gooseberry syrup, dashed through with the
flowers, was served as a cool muscatel-
flavoured drink with soda water, and to this
simplest of jams, too, the elderflowers add a
wildish note. If you can't get hold of elderflowers, make the jam without.*

4 lb (1.75 kg) gooseberries
1½ pints (900 ml) water
12 elderflower sprays
4 lb (1.75 kg) sugar

Top and tail the gooseberries and cook
slowly with the water. As soon as the
skins begin to soften, add the elderflowers in a muslin bag, with as much
green stalk removed as possible. When
the gooseberries are a pulp, add the
sugar, and boil until set. Remove the
muslin bag, pot and seal.

Marrow, Rhubarb & Ginger Jam

*This is a good jam for late summer, when
the rhubarb is fat and your marrows are
sprawled like stranded zeppelins. Vegetable
jams are not as unusual as commercial pro-
ducers would suggest; they go especially well
at a high tea.*

3 lb (1.5 kg) marrow, peeled and cubed
3 lb (1.5 kg) rhubarb, cut into short lengths
6 lb (2.75 kg) sugar
juice and rind of 3 lemons
3 oz (75 g) preserved ginger, chopped

Put the marrow and rhubarb in a large
bowl and cover with the sugar. Leave
overnight. Tip with its juice, the juice
of the lemons, and the ginger into a
preserving pan. Chop up the whole
lemon rind, tie it in a muslin bag, and
suspend it over the edge of the preserving pan. Bring the pan to the boil
and boil hard for about 30 minutes,
until setting point is reached. Remove
the muslin bag, pour into jars and seal
and label.

Gooseberry Jam

Fig Jam

Figs are almost mythically gorgeous things, a gift from Bacchus, the Romans said; and unless you are lucky enough to have a tree, this is a precious jam you are likely to make only in this rather small quantity.

3 lemons
1 lb (450 g) fresh figs
8 oz (225 g) cooking apples
1 lb (450 g) sugar

Squeeze the juice of all 3 lemons and pare the zest of one of them. Cut up the figs, and peel and slice the apples. Put into a pan with the lemon juice and zest. Cover the pan and simmer until the fruit is tender. Add the sugar and stir until it has dissolved. Then boil the jam quickly for 15 minutes, before testing for set. Pour into jars. Seal and label.

Fig Jam

Apple, Lemon & Ginger Marmalade

Another recipe to make the most of your windfalls.

5 lb (2.25 kg) cooking apples

I pint (600 ml) water

zest and juice of 3 lemons

4 oz (100 g) stem ginger, finely chopped

2 teaspoons ground ginger

4 lb (1.75 kg) sugar

Peel the apples, remove the cores and cut the flesh into quarters. Put the peelings and cores into a pan, cover with the water and boil for 20 minutes. Put the flesh of the apples into a preserving pan. Pour the water from the peelings over and boil until soft. Add the rest of the ingredients, bring to the boil again and stir until setting point is reached. Bottle as usual.

Blackcurrant & Rhubarb Jam

An unusual and beautifully coloured jam.

5 lb (2.25 kg) blackcurrants

I lb (450 g) rhubarb

3 pints (1½ litres) water

7 lb (3.5 kg) sugar

Pick the blackcurrants off their stems and cut the rhubarb across in short lengths. Put into a pan with the water and boil until the fruit is thoroughly soft, stirring all the time to ensure that the fruit doesn't burn on the bottom of the pan. When the fruit is a pulp, add the sugar and boil fast for 15 minutes but no longer, stirring all the time. It should set very quickly.

Rose Jelly

This jelly is made from the witchy crab apple and blushing rose. No exact quantities here, but keep the juice to sugar ratio in the proportions given, and you can't go wrong.

crab apples (see method)

water, to cover

granulated sugar (see method)

rose petals (see method)

caster sugar (see method)

Wash and cut up the crab apples. Put into a pan with enough water to cover. Boil until quite soft. Strain through a jelly bag. To each 1 pint (600 ml) of juice, add 1 lb (450 g) of granulated sugar. Boil quickly until the jelly sets. Crush a quantity of strongly perfumed fresh rose petals with caster sugar (about 2 cups of rose petals to 1 cup of sugar) to a powder so that the sugar absorbs the juice from the petals. Cover with the smallest quantity of water and stew gently in a covered dish in a preheated oven at 300°F (150°C, gas mark 2) for 1 hour. Strain and add to the jelly, then bring to the boil. Pot and seal.

Mint Jelly

This jelly is a staunch friend to mutton or lamb in winter.

4 lb (1.75 kg) cooking apples, roughly chopped
2 pints (1.15 litres) water
white sugar (see method)
24 fresh mint leaves
sprigs of mint, for garnish (optional)

Put the apples and water into a pan and simmer until the fruit turns to pulp, stirring frequently. Strain the pulp in a jelly bag overnight. To each 1 pint (600 ml) of juice add 1 lb (450 g) of sugar. Add the mint and boil until set. Remove the mint leaves and pot. If liked, add a fresh sprig of mint in each jar as decoration.

Tomato Jam

At the end of summer those glassy acres of tomato farms are selling vast quantities of their crop for a song. This is a recipe which evokes the hidden sweetness of the tomato.

5 lb (2.25 kg) ripe tomatoes
1½ oz (40 g) candied ginger, chopped
2 lemons, sliced
4 lb (1.75 kg) sugar

Put the tomatoes, ginger and lemons into a preserving pan and add the sugar. Cook very slowly for 2½-4 hours until quite thick. Pot and seal.

Tomato Jam

Bramble Jelly

Bramble Jelly

Nothing is so evocative of autumn as hedgerows laden with soft black fruit; and no jelly comes so deliciously from the lap of the gods. Here the jam makers have a decided advantage over idle pluckers: blackberries contain the highest amount of pectin shortly before they ripen, and the early crop makes the most flavoursome jam.

4 lb (1.75 kg) blackberries
¾ pint (450 ml) water
sugar (see method)
juice of 2 lemons

Put the blackberries and water into a preserving pan and simmer for 30 minutes, or until soft. Press through a hair sieve to extract all the juice. To

38

each 1 pint (600 ml) of juice, add 1 lb (450 g) of sugar. Put into a pan with the lemon juice, bring to the boil and boil until set. Pot and seal.

Spiced Quince Preserve

This odalisque of the fruit world bestows her favours particularly on the preserve-maker as she doesn't make good eating straight from the tree.

7 quinces
water, to cover
grated rind and juice of 4 oranges
grated rind and juice of 1 lemon
2½ lb (1.25 kg) sugar
1-inch (2.5-cm) cinnamon stick

Peel, core and cut up the quinces. Put into a preserving pan and cover with cold water. Cook until quite soft, adding more water if necessary to prevent the fruit from burning. When tender, rub through a sieve. Put the sieved fruit into a pan with the grated orange and lemon rind and juices. Add the sugar and cinnamon, and bring to the boil. Boil rapidly for 10 minutes, or until the mixture jells. Remove the cinnamon stick, and pot.

Blackberry Cheese

A fruit cheese is essentially a jam with the moisture cooked out: it requires close attention during cooking to prevent it from sticking or burning. Rather than potting in a jar, use some shallow mould – a teacup or a soup plate – so that the cheese can be turned out whole, and eaten wickedly in slices. Wrap the hot cheese in wax paper, well pressed down, and seal in cellophane. Store in a cool, dry place for 3 months before eating, then eat straightaway. Serve at room temperature.

2 lb (900 g) cooking apples
2 lb (900 g) blackberries
granulated or preserving sugar (see method)

Peel but do not core the apples; cut them up roughly. Put the fruit in a saucepan and cook very slowly, covered, until reduced to a pulp. Rub through a coarse sieve into a bowl. Measure the strained pulp and add an equal quantity of sugar. Stir over a gentle heat until the sugar has dissolved, and the mixture has thickened so that a spoon leaves an empty trail behind it. Be careful not to burn the mixture. Pour the mixture into a mould and wrap in wax paper.

Lemon Curd

Until you have tried home-made lemon curd, you have no idea how good the stuff can be – try it on bread or as a sponge-cake filling. Store the jars in the refrigerator for up to 1 month. Once opened, eat within 1 week.

8 oz (225 g) sugar lumps
2 large lemons
3 oz (75 g) butter
3 eggs, beaten

Rub the sugar lumps over the lemons so that they absorb the flavoured oil from the skin. Put the sugar lumps in the top of a double-saucepan. Add the butter. Squeeze the juice from the lemons and add this to the pan with the beaten eggs. Set the pan over barely simmering water and cook, stirring constantly, until the mixture thickens. Pour into jars and refrigerate.

Pumpkin Curd

This rich old recipe is true to the character of the golden fat-bellied pumpkin.

4 lb (1.75 g) pumpkin
4 lb (1.75 g) sugar
8 oz (225 g) butter
grated rind and juice of 4 lemons

Peel and deseed the pumpkin and cut the flesh up into cubes. Boil the pumpkin in a little water until tender, then sieve. Put into a preserving pan and add the sugar, butter and grated lemon rind and juice. Stir well and simmer for 15 minutes. Pour into jars and store in the same way as for Lemon Curd.

Dried Apricot Jam

This jam can be made all year as dried apricots have no season.

12 oz (350 g) dried apricots
3 pints (1½ litres) boiling water
2 lb (900 g) sugar
juice of 2 lemons

Wash the apricots, put them in a large bowl and pour over the boiling water. Leave for a day until the apricots are swollen and soft. Pour the apricots and soaking liquid into a preserving pan and simmer until tender. Add the sugar and lemon juice. Bring to the boil and bubble until the jam reaches setting point. Pot as usual.

Pumpkin Curd

PICKLES & CHUTNEYS

Cold dishes — ham and beef, cheese and salads — are thinner in flavour than hot ones, and are made memorable by the pickles and chutneys which accompany them. The idea here is to pack a punch of flavour into a small space, with preserved fruit and vegetables bearing a raft of delicious spicy flavours.

The glory of home-made chutney is its versatility: almost anything goes, as long as the proportions are maintained. While the grocer can offer you a dozen varieties, solemnly adjusted to the public taste, in the kitchen you can combine ingredients like twists on a Rubik's cube. Press gang your glut of courgettes, corral your green tomatoes, and make free with the spices and aromatics you really like.

Pickles and chutneys often have an oriental inspiration — *chatni* is Indian, and ketchup comes from the Chinese *koe-chiap*, a pickled fish sauce brought to Europe in the late seventeenth century. Medieval Europeans knew about spices, too; traded through the Levant, and across the Mediterranean, they made their winter stores good to eat.

In China, brides-to-be would be asked by their prospective mothers-in-law to prove their ability to make good pickles. In more liberated societies the fact remains that men really like pickles.

Courgette Chutney

Chutney can be rather murky, however delicious; but in this recipe it retains a Mediterranean dash of colour. Use yellow courgettes, if you can, or mix with green. Try substituting pumpkins or marrows for courgettes, in which case peel and deseed.

5 lb (2.5 kg) courgettes
2 lb (900 g) fresh tomatoes
1 lb (450 g) onions
10 garlic cloves, peeled
2 pints (1.5 litres) malt or white vinegar
8 oz (225 g) sultanas
4 tablespoons salt
1 tablespoon each peppercorns, allspice,
    ground ginger, coriander seeds
3 lb (1.5 kg) white sugar

Cut the courgettes into 5-mm (¼-in) rings and halve. Chop the tomatoes roughly. Chop the onion and garlic, a little more finely. Put the ingredients into a pan with 1 pint (600 ml) of vinegar, the sultanas, salt and spices, and slowly bring to a boil. In about 2 hours, when the vegetables are tender, add the remaining vinegar and the sugar and stir to dissolve. Continue cooking until the mixture thickens, and pot.

Gooseberry & Mustard Seed Chutney

A pale, translucent chutney with a mighty taste.

8 oz (225 g) mustard seed
½ oz (15 g) cayenne
2 pints (1.5 litres) malt vinegar
3 lb (1.5 kg) green gooseberries
2 lb (900 g) brown sugar
4 oz (100 g) salt
1½ lb (675 g) seedless raisins
8 oz (225 g) currants
10 garlic cloves, peeled

Wash and dry the mustard seed, and bruise it gently. Add the cayenne to the vinegar. Put the gooseberries, the mustard seed and vinegar into a preserving pan, bring to the boil and boil until tender. Add the sugar and salt, and stir until they have dissolved. Rub through a sieve. Mince the raisins and currants. Bruise the garlic thoroughly. Mix all the ingredients together, then bring back to the boil and boil briefly until the mixture is rich and thick. Pour into jars. The longer the chutney is kept, the better its flavour.

Gooseberry & Mustard Seed Chutney

Plum Relish

Plum Relish

A tasty sauce to accompany pork, duck or other rich meats or as an authentic alternative to commercially made barbecue sauce.

4 lb (1.75 kg) plums
1 pint (600 ml) vinegar
1½ lb (675 kg) brown sugar
3 teaspoons salt
4 onions
3 teaspoons crushed peppercorns
3 dried chillies
1 teaspoon cloves
2 teaspoons mixed spice

Wash the plums and discard the stalks. Put all the ingredients into a pan and cover. Bring to the boil very slowly and cook very gently for 30 minutes. Leave until cold. Remove the onions and rub through a sieve. Boil the plum mixture vigorously for 5 minutes, then bottle. Heat sterilize (see p.17), then seal tightly.

Date Chutney

For anyone who finds dates cloying, this sweet chutney is relieved by apples, ginger, mustard and cayenne, and makes a good foil for cold lamb and pork.

2 lb (900 g) cooking apples, peeled and cored
2 lb (900 g) dried dates
1 large onion
1 teaspoon each salt, mustard and ground ginger
pinch of cayenne
1 pint (600 ml) vinegar
8 oz (225 g) demerara sugar

Chop the apples roughly together with the dates and onion. Put into a preserving pan and add the spices and vinegar. Simmer until tender. Dissolve the sugar in the mixture, then return to the boil and pot.

Pumpkin Preserve

Pumpkins are ripe just when cooks are taken over by that primeval urge to lay down stores for the winter.

1½ lb (675 g) sugar
1 sliced lemon
1½ pints (900 ml) water
2 lb (900 g) pumpkins, peeled and cubed
2 tablespoons ginger in syrup, finely sliced

Put the sugar and lemon in a pan with the water and boil until it makes a thin syrup which will stick to a wooden spoon. Add the pumpkin cubes and boil vigorously for 15 minutes. Add the preserved ginger and boil for a few minutes, then pot. Heat sterilize (see p.17), then seal tightly.

Spiced Crab Apples

A recipe that doesn't mask the sharpness of this ancient apple.

4 lb (1.75 kg) crab apples
water, to cover
peel of 1 lemon, cut into strips
sugar (see method)
white wine vinegar (see method)
½ tablespoon each peppercorns and coriander seeds, ½-inch (2.5-cm) cinnamon stick, ground or crushed in a pestle and mortar

Wash the fruit, remove the stalks and cut out any blemishes. Put into a pan with enough boiling water to cover. Add strips of the lemon peel. Simmer until just tender, then strain off the cooking liquor. To each 1 pint (600 ml) of liquid, add 1 lb (450 g) of sugar, ¼ pint (150 ml) of vinegar and 1 teaspoon of the ground spices. Boil the mixture, stirring well to dissolve the sugar; then add the crab apples and simmer, uncovered, over a gentle heat until the apples are translucent and the syrup is reduced (about 40 minutes). Ladle the fruit into warmed, sterilized jars, cover with syrup, then heat sterilize (see p.17); seal tightly.

Blackberry Chutney

Blackberries have a relatively long season. The first picking makes a classic jam; the second – not so rich in pectin – could make this unusual and delicious chutney.

1 lb (450 g) cooking apples
6 onions, finely chopped
3 lb (1.5 kg) blackberries
3 oz (75 g) salt
1 oz (25 g) ground ginger
1 oz (25 g) mustard
1 teaspoon mace
1 pint (600 ml) vinegar
1 lb (450 g) demerara sugar

Peel, core and chop the apples. Put into a preserving pan with the onions, blackberries, spices and vinegar and cook for 1 hour. Add the sugar and cook for a further 2 hours. Rub through a sieve, put into jars and seal.

Pickled Walnuts

You will need freshly picked walnuts. The pickled walnuts will be good to eat in 3 months, and they will keep for 2 years.

about 100 green walnuts
salt (see method)
water (see method)
To each 2 pints (1.15 litres) of wine vinegar,
    2oz (50 g) whole black peppercorns
    1 oz (25 g) allspice
    1 oz (25 g) bruised root ginger

Prick the walnuts with a fork and soak in brine, made of 4 lb (1.75 kg) salt to each 8 pints (4.5 litres) of water, for 9 days, changing the brine every 3 days. Drain, place on a dish, and leave them in the sun for 2 or 3 days to blacken. Boil the wine vinegar with the spices for 10 minutes. Put the walnuts into jars, bring the vinegar back to the boil and pour over the walnuts to cover. Heat sterilize (see p.17), and seal.

Pickled Walnuts

Clear Tomato Relish

An unusual sharp and spicy jelly to serve with cold meats or on the side of a pilaff.

3 cloves
½ stick cinnamon
3 lb (1.5 kg) ripe tomatoes, roughly chopped
1½ pints (900 ml) water
½ pint (300 ml) malt vinegar
3 lb (1.5 kg) white sugar

Put the spices in a muslin bag and place in a pan with the tomatoes and water. Cook gently until soft. Remove the spices and rub the tomatoes through a sieve. Add the vinegar and sugar and stir to dissolve the sugar. Bring to the boil and boil until the relish reaches setting point, between 10 and 15 minutes. Pot, then heat sterilize (see p.17), then seal tightly.

Pickled Turnips

Pickled Turnips

Eat the turnip leaves fresh and make this sharp pickle with their roots.

2 lb (900 g) small white turnips
a few celery leaves
4 garlic cloves, peeled and finely chopped
1 raw beetroot, peeled and thinly sliced
4-5 tablespoons salt
1½ pints (900 ml) water
½ pint (300 ml) white wine vinegar

Peel, wash and halve or quarter the turnips. Pack into a glass jar with celery leaves and garlic, and a layer of beetroot at regular intervals. Dissolve the salt in the water, and stir in the vinegar. Pour over the vegetables in the jar. Heat sterilize (see p.17), then seal the lid tightly. Store for 10 days in a warm place (for example, near a radiator), then transfer to a cool place. Eat within 6 weeks.

Pickled Cauliflower & Red Cabbage

The pickle jar works its alchemy on these workaday vegetables.

1 cauliflower
½ red cabbage
1 or 2 dried chillies
4-5 tablespoons salt
1½ pints (900 ml) water
½ pint (300 ml) white wine vinegar

Wash the cauliflower and break it into florets. Dice the cabbage into thick chunks, cutting in one direction, then the other, without breaking the chunks up. Place alternate layers of cauliflower and cabbage in a glass jar, burying the chilli in the middle. Dissolve the salt in the water and stir in the vinegar. Cover the vegetables with the pickling liquid, then heat sterilize (see p.17) and seal the jar tightly. Store in a warm place for about 10 days, then transfer to a cool place. The pickle should be eaten within 6 weeks.

Cherry Pickle

Ripe cherries often fall from the tree before you get a chance to eat them: they arrive cheap in the shops in season, too. This pickle relies on the crisp texture of whole ripe cherries.

2 lb (900 g) ripe red cherries
I lb (450 g) sugar
For each muslin bag, pinch of allspice, pinch of mace, pinch of cinnamon, a little grated nutmeg
½ pint (300 ml) vinegar

Stone the fruit and layer them in a pan with the sugar, alternately. Between every two layers of fruit put muslin bags of the spices. Add the vinegar and boil for 5 minutes. Strain off the liquor into a pan. Pack the fruit into hot, sterilized jars. Boil the syrup until it is thick. Strain, discard the muslin bags and pour the syrup over the fruit in the jars. Heat sterilize (see p.17), then seal tightly and label.

Cherry Pickle

COUNTRY PRESERVES RECIPES

Pickled Mushrooms

Mushrooms are mysterious and flighty: their arrival can never be guaranteed. One year nothing, the next year, an embarrassment. So seize them gladly when they arrive in force, and keep them dried or pickled, as in this delicious old country recipe.

4 lb (1.75 kg) button mushrooms
2-in (5-cm) piece root ginger, sliced into
   matchsticks
½ teaspoon mace
1 teaspoon peppercorns
2 teaspoons salt
2 oz (50 g) dry mustard
vinegar (see method)

Remove the mushroom stalks, wash the heads in salted water and peel. Put into a pan with the ginger and spices and cover with vinegar. Cook in a pre-heated oven at 275°F (140°C, gas mark 1), or over a very low heat, at less than a simmer, until the mushrooms are small and soft. Spoon the mushrooms into heated jars, cover with the hot vinegar. Heat sterilize (see p.17), then seal tightly and label.

Dill Pickles

A German recipe that has powered a billion sandwiches in the United States.

generous handful of celery leaves
4 lb (1.75 kg) small pickling cucumbers
1 heaped teaspoon fresh grated horseradish
2 tablespoons fresh tarragon
several sprays of fresh dill
1 heaped tablespoon salt for every 1¾ pints
   (1 litre) cold water

Spread the celery leaves over the bottom of a large jar or crock, and pack the cucumbers in on top, interspersed with generous quantities of horseradish, tarragon and especially dill. Dissolve the salt in cold water and pour the brine to cover the cucumbers, holding them down with a weighted saucer. Cover the jar with a cloth and leave in a cool place for 10-14 days, when the pickles will emerge glossy and crisp. Refrigerate and eat within 6 weeks.

Morrocan Preserved Lemons

A taste of North Africa.

6 unwaxed lemons

3-4 tablespoons salt

1 teaspoon black peppercorns

2-inch (5-cm) cinnamon stick

½ teaspoon cloves

1 teaspoon coriander seeds

1-2 bay leaves

Cut down the lemons on four sides nearly to the bottom, the quarters still attached at one end, flower-like. Rub salt on the insides, then push them closed again. Pour a tablespoon of salt on the bottom of a preserving jar. Pack in the lemons, pushing them down and sprinkling the spices and more salt between the layers, until you reach within half an inch (2.5 cm) of the top of the jar. Press a bay leaf or two down the side so that you can see them shining through. If there isn't enough juice squeezed out of the lemons as they are packed in to cover the fruit, squeeze a further lemon or two and pour in the juice. Seal the jar and leave for at least a month, shaking the jar regularly. The lemons should be rinsed before using them.

Rhubarb Relish

For all its homely associations, rhubarb is really an Eastern vegetable, as this family recipe dating from the nineteenth century bears out.

2 lb (900 g) rhubarb

2 lb (900 g) onions, finely chopped

1 pint (600 ml) vinegar

1 tablespoon salt

3 cups brown sugar

1 teaspoon ground ginger

1 teaspoon chilli powder

1 teaspoon ground cumin

1 teaspoon allspice

1 teaspoon black pepper

Cut the rhubarb into short lengths, stringing it if necessary. Put all the ingredients together in a preserving pan and boil until soft. Bottle as usual, heat sterilize (see p.17), then seal tightly and label.

BOTTLED FRUIT & VEGETABLES

These recipes are treasured as much for their appearance as for their flavours, the fruits of summer gleaming out through pellucid liquid of mysterious colour.

Bottled fruit and vegetables make very good presents, especially fruits which are bottled in intoxicating spirits. Rhubarb, of course, is a vegetable, and only its high acid content makes it suitable for bottling; most vegetables, as a rule, are too low in natural acid to bottle safely, except in the form of pickles or jams, and are best preserved in the freezer. It is the luscious fruits that bottle best – peaches, pears, firm berries, quinces – and whose flavour and texture is actually enhanced by mellowing in syrup.

Syrup is the simplest creation in the world and very easy to make. Ordinary white sugar is melted in water by stirring over a low heat, then it is brought to the boil and simmered for a few minutes. This is all that is required. For an interesting, subtle twist, add a little cinnamon or lemon peel to the syrup at the end. After preparing the fruit and placing it in a sterilized jar, pour the syrup over the contents to cover. Shake the jar a little to release any trapped bubbles of air, screw the lid down tight and then unscrew half a turn, to make sure that the air escapes during heat sterilizing (see p.17).

Bottled Early Rhubarb

Bottled Early Rhubarb

For when the rhubarb is still pale and slender.

8 oz (225 g) sugar
1 pint (600 ml) water
rhubarb (see method)

Make a light syrup: dissolve the sugar in ½ pint (300 ml) water over a low heat until clear. Add a further ½ pint (300 ml) of cold water, and leave to cool. Cut the rhubarb to the depth of the bottle or jars, pack them in tightly, and cover with the cold syrup. Screw on the lids, and set the bottles or jars deep in a pan of water. Bring the water to a low simmer (do not let it boil), and maintain for 20 minutes to sterilize the jars. Remove the bottles or jars from the pan and screw down the lids tightly.

Preserved Quinces

The queen of fruits with the prince of herbs.

3 lb (1.5 kg) quinces
water, to cover
juice of ½ lemon
3 lb (1.5 kg) sugar
a few sprigs of basil

Peel and core the quinces, and cut into ¼-in (¾-cm) segments with a stainless steel knife. Soak overnight in acidulated water (with lemon juice added) in an earthenware pot. Put the quinces and water into a preserving pan. Bring to the boil, then simmer until the quinces soften and turn pink. Remove from the heat for 10 minutes, then add the sugar and boil hard. In 10 minutes or so the fruit reddens and turns transparent: the syrup is at setting point. Add a few sprigs of basil and pot. Heat sterilize (see p.17), then seal tightly.

Chilli Oil

A simple-flavoured oil that gives an oriental dash to hot or cold food. The longer it keeps, the hotter it becomes.

1 tablespoon dried red chillies
1 pint (600 ml) sunflower oil

Smash the chillies on a board with a heavy knife, or in a mortar. Place in a clean, dry bottle and fill to the brim with oil. Seal, shake well, and store for up to a month in a cool, dark place before using.

Peppers in Oil

*Use a few yellow and orange peppers
among the more flavoursome red ones –
flamenco colours in a big glass jar.*

4 lb (1.75 kg) sweet red peppers
a few bay leaves
handful of peppercorns
4 garlic cloves, peeled
1 teaspoon salt
1 tablespoon coriander
olive oil (see method)

Roast the bell peppers until the skins
are black. Remove the skins, and
extract the cores and seeds. Put the
peppers in a bowl, cover with vinegar
and leave to soak for 30 minutes. Wipe
the peppers with a damp cloth. Pack
into a big glass jar with bay leaves, a
small handful of peppercorns, the garlic, salt and coriander seeds. Cover
with olive oil and seal. Refrigerate and
eat within 1 week.

Peppers in Oil

Brandied Peaches

Brandied Peaches
A Christmas present to yourself.

4 lb (1.75 kg) peaches
4 lb (1.75 kg) sugar
1 pint (600 ml) brandy

Make a syrup: put the sugar in saucepan with just enough water to dissolve the sugar over a low heat. Bring to boiling point and add the peaches, halved and stoned. Cook slowly until the peaches are tender. Peel off the skins and transfer the fruit to jars with a slotted spoon. Boil the syrup for another 20 minutes or so, until it is well-thickened. Stir in the brandy and pour over the fruit. Heat sterilize (see p.17), then seal tightly and store in a cool, dry place.

Sloe Gin
Sloes ripen from the end of late summer. Pick them with the bloom still on them. The gin – a rich red cordial – arrives in perfect time for Christmas.

8 oz (225 g) ripe sloes
22 fl oz (700 ml) bottle of gin
8 oz (225 g) granulated sugar

Prick the sloes all over with a clean knitting needle and add to the gin. Cork the bottle and leave for 2 months. Strain off the sloes and throw them away. Add the sugar and keep for at least 6 weeks before drinking.

Berries in Liquor
This pudding was brought back to Germany by troops stationed in China before World War I. Once the jar is on the go, any fresh berries in season may be added, with a little sprinkling of fresh sugar, provided that the liquor is topped up to keep them covered.

rye whiskey, Scotch whisky, or vodka
sugar (see method)
seasonal berries, such as strawberries,
    blackberries, currants, greengages and
    grapes, or green walnuts spiked with cloves
2-inch (5-cm) cinnamon stick
2-inch (5-cm) piece of vanilla pod

Half-fill a huge jar or crock with the liquor. Stir in sugar until no more will dissolve. Pack in unbruised, unblemished berries, tucking the cinnamon and vanilla into the centre. Stopper tightly and leave for a month before eating – and drinking.

Apple, lemon and ginger
   marmalade, 36

Berries in liquor, 63
Blackberry cheese, 39
Blackberry chutney, 48
Blackcurrant and rhubarb
   jam, 36
Bottling techniques 17
Bramble jelly, 38

Cauliflower and red cabbage,
   pickled, 51
Cherry pickle, 51
Chilli oil, 59
Chopping board, 12
Chutney
   blackberry, 48
   courgette, 44
   date, 47
   gooseberry and mustard
      seed, 44
   versatility, 43
Clear tomato relish, 51
Courgette chutney, 44
Crab apples, spiced, 48

Date chutney, 47
Dill pickles, 54
Dried apricot jam, 40

Equipment, 10-14

Fig jam, 35

Gooseberry and mustard seed
   chutney, 44
Gooseberry jam, 32
Grapefruit marmalade, 31

Ingredients, preparing, 18
Jam thermometers, 12, 28
Jams
   blackcurrant and rhubarb,
      36
   dried apricot, 40
   fig, 35
   gooseberry, 32
   marrow, rhubarb and gin-
      ger, 32
   setting, 28
   tomato, 37
Jars, 13, 14
   cleanliness, 17
   labels, 24
   lids, 24
   presentation, 24
   saving, 21
   sealing, 17, 21, 22
   shapes, 21
Jellies, 28
   bramble, 38
   mint, 37
   rose, 36

Knives, 12, 13

Labels, 24
Ladles, 12
Lemon curd, 40

Marmalade
   apple, lemon and ginger, 36
   grapefruit, 31
   Seville, 31
Marrow, rhubarb and ginger
   jam, 32
Mint jelly, 37
Moroccan preserved lemons, 55

Mushrooms, pickled, 54
Muslin, 12
Paring knives, 13
Peaches, brandies, 63
Pectin, 28
Peppers in oil, 60
Plum relish, 47
Preserves
   glut, dealing with, 14
   keeping dry and cool, 23
Preserving pans, 10
Preserving sugar, 18
Preserving, art of, 6
Pumpkin curd, 40
Pumpkin preserve, 47

Quince preserve, spiced, 39
Quinces, preserved, 59

Rhubarb relish, 55
Rhubarb, bottled early, 59
Rose jelly, 36

Scales, 10
Sealing jars, 17, 21, 22
Seville marmalade, 31
Sieves, 12
Sloe gin, 63
Spiced crab apples, 48
Spiced quince preserve, 39
Spices, 18
Sterilization, 17
Storage times, 23

Tomato jam, 37
Turnips, pickled, 49

Walnuts, pickled, 49
Wooden spoons, 10